M000211229

PURSUE

Lifeway Students

Published by Lifeway Press® • © 2021 Fellowship of Christian Athletes

ISBN: 978-1-0877-2722-6

Item: 005828665

Dewey Decimal Classification Number: 248.83

Subject Heading: RELIGION/ CHRISTIAN MINISTRY/ YOUTH

Printed in the United States of America.

Student Ministry Publishing
Lifeway Resources
One Lifeway Plaza
Nashville, Tennessee 37234

We believe that the Bible has God for its author; salvation for its end; and truth, without any mixture of error, for its matter and that all Scripture is totally true and trustworthy. To review Lifeway's doctrinal guideline, please visit www.lifeway.com/doctrinalguideline.

TABLE OF CONTENTS

GET TO KNOW FCA

The Fellowship of Christian Athletes is touching millions of lives one heart at a time. Since 1954, FCA has been challenging coaches and athletes on the professional, college, high school, junior high and youth levels to use the powerful platform of sport to reach every coach and every athlete with the transforming power of Jesus Christ. FCA focuses on serving local communities around the globe by engaging, equipping and empowering coaches and athletes to unite, inspire and change the world through the gospel.

VISION

To see the world transformed by Jesus Christ through the influence of coaches and athletes.

MISSION

To lead every coach and athlete into a growing relationship with Jesus Christ and His church.

VALUES

Integrity, Serving, Teamwork, Excellence

For more information about FCA, visit FCA.org.

HOW TO USE

In this book, you will find eight weeks of group sessions and twenty days of devos. There are also some useful tips included in the back of this study to use during group time.

GROUP SESSIONS

Each group session uses the following format to facilitate simple yet meaningful interaction among group members along with the lessons presented in this study.

WARM-UP. This page includes questions to get the conversation started and to introduce the main teaching. After discussing the questions, consider watching the short introduction videos to kick off your workout.

WORKOUT. Using biblical truth to apply to life as a competitor, this section includes questions and statements to help student athletes learn what it takes to pursue God.

WRAP UP. In this section, students will see how Scripture applies to their everyday lives and calls for their dedication to Jesus and His ministry.

OVERTIME. This is a chance for students to further engage the group session and play with the topic on their own. Encourage students to complete the activity on their own and discuss it the following week.

PERSONAL DEVOS

TRAINING TIME. There are twenty personal devos at the end of this study. Encourage students to begin a habit of daily study over the weeks following your time together. Each devo includes a short teaching, followed by a few questions and Scripture passages to continue their exploration.

SESSION 1

PURSUE
TRUTH

"And you will know the truth, and the truth will set you free."

John 8:32

Q: What athletic pursuit is most important to you right now?

Q: How much time do you spend each day working toward that goal?

Q: What would achieving your athletic pursuits mean to you?

● WATCH SESSION 1 VIDEO

WORKOUT

LOOKING FOR THE TRUTH

In Luke 19:1-10, we read about a man named Zacchaeus, a tax collector who cheated the people in Jericho and became very wealthy. At that time, Jesus had gained a reputation as a great teacher and miracle worker. Zacchaeus wanted to catch a glimpse of Jesus, but his short stature made it difficult for him to see over the crowd. So, he climbed into a tree and waited for Jesus to walk past.

> *When Jesus came by, he looked up at Zacchaeus and called him by name. "Zacchaeus!" he said. "Quick, come down! I must be a guest in your home today." Zacchaeus quickly climbed down and took Jesus to his house in great excitement and joy. But the people were displeased. "He has gone to be the guest of a notorious sinner," they grumbled. Meanwhile, Zacchaeus stood before the Lord and said, "I will give half my wealth to the poor, Lord, and if I have cheated people on their taxes, I will give them back four times as much!" Jesus responded, "Salvation has come to this home today, for this man has shown himself to be a true son of Abraham. For the Son of Man came to seek and save those who are lost" (Luke 19:5-10).*

Zacchaeus pursued truth and found a new path to fulfillment. Once he caught a glimpse of Jesus, his wealth no longer mattered in light of the eternal treasure the Son of God offered him.

Q: In what ways can you relate to Zacchaeus's story?

Q: Describe a time when you have done things out of the ordinary to pursue truth. What was the result of that pursuit?

KNOW THE WHAT

When we're pursuing big dreams, close relationships, or material things, we can easily let our pursuit drive our focus, actions, behaviors, and priorities. That's not necessarily a bad thing, but what if pursuing those things ultimately isn't healthy or isn't good for us in the long run?

That's why it's important that we "know the what," or understand what we really need in our lives. The Bible is clear about what that is—a relationship with Jesus Christ. It was Jesus who explained why this is so important while teaching His followers:

> *Jesus told him, "I am the way, the truth, and the life. No one can come to the Father except through me" (John 14:6).*

A few chapters earlier, Jesus revealed why it is so important to pursue truth.

> *"And you will know the truth, and the truth will set you free" (John 8:32).*

In other words, Jesus was saying living out truth sets us free from empty pursuits, the pressure to perform, the desire to please others, and the guilt and shame of our sin.

In a world where nothing seems to be certain, we can trust that God's Word is the absolute truth and never changes. Here are just a few truths we can hold onto:

- God created us in His image (Gen. 1:27).
- We were all born sinners, separated from God (Rom. 3:23; 5:12).
- God sent His Son Jesus to die for our sins (John 3:16).
- Salvation is available for anyone who repents of their sins and accepts Christ as their Lord and Savior (Rom. 10:9).
- God has a purpose and plan for everyone (John 15:16).
- There is a place called heaven where those who trust and believe in Christ will spend eternity (John 14:2-3).

While these are only a fraction of the truths we find in the Bible, we can experience more great truths as we dive into God's Word.

Q: Why are material pursuits temporary?

Q: When you pursue material things, do you feel satisfied with what you have, or do you feel the need for something more?

Q: Which one of the truths listed above resonates with you the most? Which one do you struggle to believe?

WRAP UP

If you're tired of pursuing material things that don't last, consider these three steps that will help you pursue the ultimate truth that can only be found in the gospel of Jesus Christ:

1. **Read the Truth:** First and foremost, you must believe that the Bible is truly the living, breathing Word of God. Then, be intentional about studying the Bible daily.

   For the word of God is alive and powerful. It is sharper than the sharpest two-edged sword, cutting between soul and spirit, between joint and marrow. It exposes our innermost thoughts and desires (Heb. 4:12).

2. **Pray the Truth:** Ask God to forgive your sins and invite Jesus to come into your heart and rule as Lord over your life.

   If you openly declare that Jesus is Lord and believe in your heart that God raised him from the dead, you will be saved (Rom. 10:9).

3. **Reach for Truth:** Find a community of Christians who can help you grow closer to God and in your relationship with Him.

   "Physical training is good, but training for godliness is much better, promising benefits in this life and in the life to come" (1 Tim. 4:8).

OVERTIME

It's not difficult to identify the things we're pursuing as athletes. Victories, championships, records, scholarships, and professional contracts are very tangible. But sometimes we need to step back to see the big picture of what we really want for our lives.

Below is a list of common pursuits. In the space provided, determine which of these things you spend the most time pursuing (1 = never, 10 = always).

Acceptance _____

Achievement _____

Community _____

Education _____

Fame _____

Love _____

Popularity _____

Position _____

Power _____

Relationships _____

Security _____

Significance _____

Wealth _____

Q: Review your list and look at the three things that you spend the most time pursuing. What is the driving force behind your pursuit of those things?

Q: What are you currently doing to pursue those things?

Q: How do you expect your life to change once you attain the things you are pursuing?

Flip to page 78 and go through "The FOUR." If you haven't already committed your heart to Christ, talk to your coach or adult leader about making that game-changing decision today.

PURSUE FAITH

"Faith shows the reality of what we hope for; it is the evidence of things we cannot see."

Hebrews 11:1

Q: When you're training, practicing, or preparing for a competition, what gives you the belief that your hard work is going to pay off?

Q: Who or what do you put your faith in as an athlete?

● WATCH SESSION 2 VIDEO

WORKOUT

AMAZING FAITH

Have you ever believed something incredible was about to unfold? Maybe it was a time when your star teammate stepped into action with the game on the line. Or, it might have been an instance when your coach called a play that your opponents could never stop. Perhaps it was simply a time when everything was going your way and you had that feeling of invincibility.

In those moments, faith can give us the belief that there will be a favorable result even before it happens. Such was the case with a Roman military officer who came to Jesus with an urgent request:

> *"Lord, my young servant lies in bed, paralyzed and in terrible pain." Jesus said, "I will come and heal him." But the officer said, "Lord, I am not worthy to have you come into my home. Just say the word from where you are, and my servant will be healed... When Jesus heard this, he was amazed. Turning to those who were following him, he said, "I tell you the truth, I haven't seen faith like this in all Israel!"...Then Jesus said to the Roman officer, "Go back home. Because you believed, it has happened." And the young servant was healed that same hour (Matt. 8:6-8,10,13).*

The Son of God's reputation as a miracle worker was spreading across the region. That gave the Roman officer the faith to surrender his need to Jesus even while others were struggling to believe what they were seeing with their own eyes.

Q: What does the word "faith" mean to you as an athlete?

Q: Do you generally consider yourself to be someone who has a strong faith in God, so-so faith, or not much faith?

Q: What events in your life might be causing your current level of faith in God?

KNOW THE HOW

Faith is a key component in an athlete's life. It's even more important for the Christ follower. Faith has to be rooted in something true. False beliefs or wishful thinking rarely lead to favorable results. That's why it's vital to understand how purpose and meaning are fulfilled in our lives.

The first step is acknowledging one of the most basic, yet powerful biblical truths, spoken directly by Jesus Himself:

> *Jesus told him, "I am the way, the truth, and the life. No one can come to the Father except through me" (John 14:6).*

Jesus is the only way we can be redeemed back to a relationship with God, but our Faith in Him is also how we find the purpose and meaning God has planned for us.

The next step is surrendering that purpose and meaning to God and trusting Him to guide us in using the gifts, talents, and desires He has given us. Part of that process is recognizing our limited ability to change circumstances and allowing God to do the work He has said He will do.

> *Let us strip off every weight that slows us down, especially the sin that so easily trips us up. And let us run with endurance the race God has set before us. We do this by keeping our eyes on Jesus, the champion who initiates and perfects our faith. Because of the joy awaiting him, he endured the cross, disregarding its shame. Now he is seated in the place of honor beside God's throne (Heb. 12:1b-2).*

That doesn't mean we are to stop doing what we've been called to do. In fact, the Bible never tells us to stop doing good or walking out our mission (see James 2:17). Instead, we should stop worrying about how things are going to happen and what the results are going to be and let God take care of the details. That's what faith is really all about.

> *Faith shows the reality of what we hope for; it is the evidence of things we cannot see (Heb. 11:1).*

Q: List a few things that tend to shake your faith as an athlete. What steps do you usually take to get back on track? What shakes your faith as a Christ follower? How do you restore that faith?

Q: What are some things that you need to surrender to God as a show of your faith and trust in His plan and purpose for your life?

WRAP UP

Our circumstances and the things we look to for help are temporary. God is forever. Faith is looking to Him as our source. Here are three key things to pursuing faith and stepping out into the purpose God has for our lives:

1. **Stop:** Recognize that Jesus already did the hard work for us. He sacrificially gave His life for us on the cross, defeated the power of death when He rose from the grave, and sent His Holy Spirit to guide our steps and give us the strength to overcome any adversity we might face.

   By his divine power, God has given us everything we need for living a godly life. We have received all of this by coming to know him, the one who called us to himself by means of his marvelous glory and excellence. And because of his glory and excellence, he has given us great and precious promises. These are the promises that enable you to share his divine nature and escape the world's corruption caused by human desires (2 Pet. 1:3-4).

2. **Surrender:** Give up anything that is holding you back—those things that you really can't control and the sinful behaviors that are keeping you from experiencing the fullness of a relationship with God.

   So humble yourselves under the mighty power of God, and at the right time he will lift you up in honor. Give all your worries and cares to God, for he cares about you (1 Pet. 5:6-7).

3. **Start:** We need to do our part and keep walking out the path that has been laid before us. But ultimately, our action is meant to activate our faith and show God that we trust Him to complete the work He started in us and the purpose He gave us before we were even born.

   So let's not get tired of doing what is good. At just the right time we will reap a harvest of blessing if we don't give up (Gal. 6:9).

   And I am certain that God, who began the good work within you, will continue his work until it is finally finished on the day when Christ Jesus returns (Phil. 1:6).

OVERTIME

We use the word "faith" a lot, but it's come to have several different meanings. There are a lot of people, things, and ideals that we might have a great deal of faith in or not much faith at all. Take a few moments to rank how much faith you have in some of the things listed below (1 = zero faith; 10 = 100 percent faith).

Achievements   _____

Athletes/Celebrities _____

Friends   _____

God   _____

Money   _____

Parents   _____

Politicians   _____

Relatives   _____

Teachers   _____

Yourself   _____

Q: What are some other ways that people might use the word "faith"?

Q: Which item on the list do you have the least amount of faith in? Why?

Q: Which item do you have the most amount of faith in? Why?

Q: What rank did you give your faith in God? If it's not already, how can you begin to get closer to having 100 percent faith in Him?

PURSUE LIFE

"The thief's purpose is to steal and kill and destroy. My purpose is to give them a rich and satisfying life."

John 10:10

Q: What are some things athletes might do while pursuing their goals that are unhealthy, unethical, or harmful to themselves or others?

Q: How would you feel if you achieved all of your goals but ended up hurting yourself or others along the way?

WATCH SESSION 3 VIDEO

WORKOUT

LOOKING FOR LOVE

One of the key components to having a good life is experiencing love. We desire many aspects of love—from our family, friends, or our significant other.

Relational love can be found all throughout the Bible. But perhaps no story better captures the spirit of that pursuit and its potential downfall than the story of Jesus and the Samaritan woman found in John 4.

In those times, Jewish people did not associate with Samaritans; yet Jesus was sitting next to a well when this Samaritan woman approached to get some water. Much to her surprise, Jesus asked her if she could get him a drink. Why would He do this?

> *Jesus replied, "If you only knew the gift God has for you and who you are speaking to, you would ask me, and I would give you living water" (v. 10).*

Still struggling to understand, the woman had more questions to which Jesus replied:

> *Jesus replied, "Anyone who drinks this water will soon become thirsty again. But those who drink the water I give will never be thirsty again. It becomes a fresh, bubbling spring within them, giving them eternal life" (vv. 13-14).*

That's when things got really interesting.

> *"Please, sir," the woman said, "give me this water! Then I'll never be thirsty again, and I won't have to come here to get water." "Go and get your husband," Jesus told her. "I don't have a husband," the woman replied. Jesus said, "You're right! You don't have a husband—for you have had five husbands, and you aren't even married to the man you're living with now. You certainly spoke the truth!" (vv. 15-18).*

Just like athletes who cut corners or employ an "at all costs" mentality, the Samaritan woman found herself jumping from one relationship to the next and making objectionable choices in hopes of experiencing real love and real life. Jesus understood exactly what was going on inside her heart. He knew that despite all of her attempts, she had never found that one thing that truly made her feel full of life. Jesus was there to show her that true life and true love could be found in a relationship with Him.

Q: The Samaritan woman was looking for fulfillment in life through relationships. How can you relate?

Q: What do you think Jesus meant when He told her He would give her "living water"?

KNOW THE WHY

If we are pursuing goals based on harmful motivations, then achieving those goals will never result in true fulfillment. Sure, there might be short-term value, but the wrong motivations might be an indicator that we are simply trying to replace something much bigger that's missing in our hearts. Those negative "whys" are not from God, but instead are from an enemy who doesn't want us to experience the fullness of life.

| *"The thief's purpose is to steal and kill and destroy" (John 10:10a).*

Satan wants us to be all wrapped up in guilt, shame, hurt, pain, and the pressure to perform in search of approval. He tempts us with pleasure and desires that can only hurt us in the long run. Even when we have good pursuits, he uses lies and deceit to taint our motivations with selfishness, greed, and pride.

Is it possible that a better life awaits us? Is it possible that there's a better path that God has laid out for each and every one of us? God's Word answers that question with a resounding, "Yes!"

| *"My purpose is to give them a rich and satisfying life" (John 10:10b).*

Changing our "what" is a big part of understanding what Jesus is talking about, but changing our "why" is the key to truly unlocking the door to that abundant life.

Q: Is it possible to have healthy goals but impure motives for reaching them? Explain.

Q: What do you think Jesus means when He talks about a "rich and satisfying life"? What would that look like for you personally?

WRAP UP

If you're tired of being consumed with unhealthy motivations that drive you into meaningless pursuits, consider these three things that will help you pursue the abundant life that can be found in a relationship with Jesus Christ:

1. **Open Your Heart:** The first step in pursuing your new life in Christ is to be open to the possibility that your motivations might be pushing you in the wrong direction.

   Search me, O God, and know my heart; test me and know my anxious thoughts. Point out anything in me that offends you, and lead me along the path of everlasting life (Ps. 139:23-24).

2. **Examine Your Heart:** Be honest with yourself. Take a look deep inside your heart and examine your motivations. Which "whys" are driving the pursuit of your goals? More importantly, allow God to examine your heart so He can reveal to you what needs to change.

   Put me on trial, Lord, and cross-examine me. Test my motives and my heart (Ps. 26:2).

3. **Surrender Your Heart:** Give your pursuits and your motivations to Jesus. Ask Him to give you new pursuits, and if your pursuits are right and good, ask Him to give you pure motives for achieving those things.

   We can make our own plans, but the Lord gives the right answer. People may be pure in their own eyes, but the Lord examines their motives. Commit your actions to the Lord, and your plans will succeed (Prov. 16:1-3).

OVERTIME

Going back to our first session, we talked about the importance of knowing what you are pursuing athletically and personally. Today, let's talk about the deeper reasons behind that pursuit. After all, that is often the burning question that goes much deeper than the "what." Answering "the why" is what this really comes down to.

Think back to the pursuits we discussed in the first session. Now, using the spaces provided below, rate each of the possible reasons why you are pursuing the things from that list (1 = not at all, 10 = major driving force).

Approval   _____

Guilt   _____

Insecurity   _____

Love   _____

Pain   _____

Pleasure   _____

Pressure   _____

Pride   _____

Purpose   _____

Shame   _____

Q: Review your list and look at the top three things that are driving your pursuits. Would you say that those things are helpful or harmful to you in the long run?

Q: How do you think your life would change if you replaced those harmful motivators with ones that were positive, healthy, and helpful?

Find a quiet place alone or with another person you can trust, and discuss the reasons behind your most passionate pursuits. Devise a plan that will help you better understand the "why" and how to surrender those passions to Christ every day.

Also, take time to download the Pursue Reading Plan on YouVersion. You can download the YouVersion Bible app in the App Store or go to Bible.com. If you are not able to directly download the reading plan, search for "Pursue" in the "Find Plan" section of the Bible app or on Bible.com.

PURSUE IDENTITY

"For we are God's masterpiece. He has created us anew in Christ Jesus, so we can do the good things he planned for us long ago."

Ephesians 2:10

Q: How do you first describe yourself when you meet someone new (e.g., athlete, student, member of a family, etc.)?

Q: How important is it for others to know that you're an athlete and/or know about your athletic accomplishments? Explain.

● **WATCH SESSION 4 VIDEO**

WORKOUT

NAME CHANGER

The Book of Acts tells the story of how the Church was born and how the first Christians worked to share the gospel with the world. It was an exciting time of exponential growth and astounding miracles, but not everyone was happy about those efforts.

A man named Saul was among the most vocal dissenters. Saul had many identifiers. His job as a skilled tentmaker was perhaps one of the least important. Saul, instead, was most proud of his race (Hebrew), religion (Judaism), citizenship (Roman), and education (theological). His pride in those aspects of his life drove him to become a religious zealot—someone who was fanatical about their religious beliefs and unwilling to change their political views against the Roman Empire.

Saul was so consumed by his mission—stopping the spread of Christianity—that he didn't even realize he was actually opposing the God he claimed to serve. But God had a plan to use Saul for a greater purpose. To get Saul on the right path, however, required a dramatic, life-changing event—an event that can be found in Acts 9.

While traveling to Damascus on a mission to arrest the Christians there, a powerful light appeared from the sky blinding Saul. God called down to Saul and told him to go into the city where he would be told what to do next.

Saul could have dug his heels in deeper. He could have resisted God's call on his life and continued to let pride guide his steps. Instead, he obeyed the Lord and received instruction from a Christian in Damascus named Ananias, who also prayed for Saul's sight to be restored.

> And immediately he began preaching about Jesus in the synagogues, saying, "He is indeed the Son of God!" (Acts 9:20).

Saul went through one of the most radical transformations recorded in the Bible. He changed his name to Paul and took on a new cause, a new faith, and a new mission. After finding his identity in Christ, Paul became the most influential Christian missionary of all time and wrote nearly one-third of the New Testament. His writings continue to help others discover that their true identity is also found in a relationship with Jesus.

Q: Go back and review Saul's different identifiers, none of which were inherently bad. In what ways can good identity traits still lead someone to take bad actions?

Q: List a few of the negative consequences of allowing good identity traits consume you.

KNOW THE YOU

Whatever is most important to us at the moment is usually the part of our identity that we focus the majority of our energy on. As an athlete, that often means talking about the sports we play, the teams we play on, the results of our latest competitions, and our personal and team accomplishments.

While certain identity traits will remain the same over time, many of them, such as what we do and where we live, will likely change. Those material things attached to our identities are temporary. Our competitive lives end, our accomplishments fade, and we have to deal with the inevitable realities of getting older.

Ironically, it was Paul—a man who was fixated on his identity early in life—who became the greatest teacher on the difficult concept. He understood that he really didn't start living until that miraculous encounter with Jesus.

> *My old self has been crucified with Christ. It is no longer I who live, but Christ lives in me. So I live in this earthly body by trusting in the Son of God, who loved me and gave himself for me (Gal. 2:20).*
>
> *This means that anyone who belongs to Christ has become a new person. The old life is gone; a new life has begun! (2 Cor. 5:17).*

The good news is that God actually gave us those identity traits that make us unique. God gave us our personalities, our talents, our abilities, and even our physical traits, so we could glorify, worship, and tell the world about Him.

> *For we are God's masterpiece. He has created us anew in Christ Jesus, so we can do the good things he planned for us long ago (Eph. 2:10).*

Q: List your identity traits. How has God already begun using your identity traits or might begin using them in the future for His purposes?

Q: What do you think Paul means when he writes, "My old self has been crucified with Christ"? What might that look like in your life?

WRAP UP

Just like Paul, we can all struggle with an identity crisis at times. But the solution is simple and can be discovered in three intentional and powerful steps:

1. **Change Your Mind:** To truly embrace your new identity in Christ, you have to learn who you really are through reading God's Word. You have to believe that what He says about you is true.

   Don't copy the behavior and customs of this world, but let God transform you into a new person by changing the way you think. Then you will learn to know God's will for you, which is good and pleasing and perfect (Rom. 12:2).

2. **Change Your Heart:** Once you've received the knowledge of who you are in Christ, allow that truth to seep into your heart and let the transformation process begin.

   Create in me a clean heart, O God. Renew a loyal spirit within me. Do not banish me from your presence, and don't take your Holy Spirit from me. Restore to me the joy of your salvation, and make me willing to obey you (Ps. 51:10-12).

3. **Change Your Life:** As the knowledge of who you are in Christ transforms your heart, everything about your life will also begin to change—your speech, your behavior, your attitude toward yourself and others, and so on.

   Since you have heard about Jesus and have learned the truth that comes from him, throw off your old sinful nature and your former way of life, which is corrupted by lust and deception. Instead, let the Spirit renew your thoughts and attitudes. Put on your new nature, created to be like God—truly righteous and holy (Eph. 4:21-24).

Identity is something we all struggle with at different times in our lives, and it often requires an assessment of our priorities to help us gain greater understanding.

Using the space below, list the 10 most important pieces of your identity. To the right of each, rank those identity traits from 1 to 10 (1 = most important, 10 = least important).

1.

2.

3.

4.

5.

6.

7.

8.

9.

10.

Q: Why are the top things on your list so important to you?

Q: Which identity traits do you think should be higher on your list?

Q: What are some things you can do today that will help you re-prioritize the parts of your identity that deserve more of your attention? How do you think that will better equip you to live out the purpose God has for your life?

PURSUE GROWTH

"Physical training is good, but training for godliness is much better, promising benefits in this life and in the life to come."

1 Timothy 4:8

Q: How important is training to your athletic success?

Q: What are some specific things you do during training and how do those efforts benefit your athletic growth?

WATCH SESSION 5 VIDEO

WORKOUT

TRAINING TIME

There are many ways athletes can approach training. Sometimes, we find ourselves working alone at home or in the gym. But it helps to have opportunities to train with a peer who can encourage and keep us accountable, or a mentor who can guide our efforts and bring out the best of us.

The same is true when we're talking about spiritual training. The apostle Timothy is a great example of this. Timothy was a young Christian who was first mentioned in Acts 16. He received training at home from his mother and grandmother and grew as a faithful member of his church body.

Timothy also gained knowledge and wisdom during his unique opportunity to accompany Paul and Silas during some of their travels. He went from trainee (as a young man under Paul's mentoring) to partner (with Paul and Silas) to leader (as a pastor at his home church).

After parting ways, Paul continued to mentor Timothy through a series of letters that can be found in the New Testament—including this well-known passage, which was written when Paul was in prison for preaching the gospel.

> *This is why I remind you to fan into flames the spiritual gift God gave you when I laid my hands on you. For God has not given us a spirit of fear and timidity, but of power, love, and self-discipline (2 Tim. 1:6-7).*

Paul was reminding Timothy that his success as a Christian leader would require continued growth, and that growth would take place as he trained or "fanned into flames" the spiritual gift God had given him.

Q: Who are some of the people you rely on to help you with your training, and how do they help you accomplish your athletic goals?

Q: In what ways do you think Timothy's training helped him grow into a dynamic Christian leader?

KNOW THE WAY

> *"Physical training is good, but training for godliness is much better, promising benefits in this life and in the life to come" (1 Tim. 4:8).*

Just like training helps us in our athletic pursuits, there is a pathway to our spiritual growth as followers of Christ. Paul laid out that path for Timothy and the other early Christians through three key disciplines: Bible reading, prayer, and Christian fellowship.

Timothy's mother and grandmother laid the foundation during his younger years, but Paul continued to teach him to stay rooted and grounded in the Word of God.

> *All Scripture is inspired by God and is useful to teach us what is true and to make us realize what is wrong in our lives. It corrects us when we are wrong and teaches us to do what is right. God uses it to prepare and equip his people to do every good work (2 Tim. 3:16-17).*

Paul also taught Timothy and many other early Christians about the power of prayer.

> *Don't worry about anything; instead, pray about everything. Tell God what you need, and thank him for all he has done. Then you will experience God's peace, which exceeds anything we can understand. His peace will guard your hearts and minds as you live in Christ Jesus (Phil. 4:6-7).*

And perhaps one of the most important ways Timothy trained was through his personal interaction with wise and godly church leaders—something Paul commonly encouraged believers to do throughout his writings.

> *Let us think of ways to motivate one another to acts of love and good works. And let us not neglect our meeting together, as some people do, but encourage one another, especially now that the day of his return is drawing near (Heb. 10:24-25).*

Q: Which disciplines (Bible reading, prayer, Christian community) do you actively make a part of your spiritual training? How have they helped you grow as a believer?

Q: Which areas of your spiritual training are more inconsistent? Why do you struggle with those disciplines? What might help you improve in those areas?

WRAP UP

Just like in our athletic training, we will never reach our fullest potential as followers of Christ without the disciplines that are vital to our spiritual development. Here are three key ways we can pursue growth and be all that God has called us to be:

1. **Grow in the Word:** The Bible tells us the truth about who God is, who God says we are, and what God says about our relationship with Him.

   For the word of God is alive and powerful. It is sharper than the sharpest two-edged sword, cutting between soul and spirit, between joint and marrow. It exposes our innermost thoughts and desires (Heb. 4:12).

2. **Grow in Prayer:** A devoted follower of Christ will take time throughout the day to seek God in prayer, listen for His voice, and receive revelation about what he or she has read in God's Word.

   Confess your sins to each other and pray for each other so that you may be healed. The earnest prayer of a righteous person has great power and produces wonderful results (James 5:16).

3. **Grow in Community:** We can't do this alone. There is immeasurable value in learning from experienced believers and praying and serving together.

   He makes the whole body fit together perfectly. As each part does its own special work, it helps the other parts grow, so that the whole body is healthy and growing and full of love (Eph. 4:16).

OVERTIME

You can't be a successful athlete without meaningful physical training. To illustrate this, use the five blank spaces below to list the most important exercises you use for physical and sport-specific development:

1. _____
2. _____
3. _____
4. _____
5. _____

Q: Which exercise is the most important part of your physical training? Why?

Q: Review your list and explain how eliminating each item might hinder your physical and sport-specific development.

As we read earlier in 1 Timothy 4:8, spiritual training is even more important than physical training because it brings benefits "in this life and in the life to come." Let's repeat the activity from above, but this time, list the most important disciplines a believer might use for spiritual development:

1. _____
2. _____
3. _____
4. _____
5. _____

Q: Which one discipline do you find easiest to make a consistent part of your daily routine? Which is most difficult and why?

Q: Go back over your list and explain how each discipline might help your spiritual development.

PURSUE TEAM

"Let us think of ways to motivate one another to acts of love and good works. And let us not neglect our meeting together, as some people do, but encourage one another, especially now that the day of his return is drawing near."

Hebrews 10:24-25

_____

Q: List some examples of why teammates are so important in your sport. If it's not a team sport, why is it important to have others around to help you succeed?

Q: What are some characteristics of a good teammate?

• WATCH SESSION 6 VIDEO

WORKOUT

GREATEST TEAM EVER

The concept of team transcends sports and is highlighted in many ways throughout the Bible. Perhaps one of the greatest teams ever assembled can be found in the Book of Acts. The original group was 12 men (or disciples) who chose to follow Jesus and learn the truth from Him.

Even though they were ordinary people, they spent three years learning from the Son of God. You might say this was the greatest team ever because their leader was and still is the greatest Coach ever.

And even though the disciples didn't truly begin to shine until Jesus left Earth, there was a reason why they were chosen to walk alongside Him throughout His ministry. Jesus had a plan but needed to train and disciple them before they could begin their greater mission.

Q: What's more important to you: having a great coach or having great teammates?

Q: What does it look like when you have both?

Q: What advantages do you think the disciples had as a team because of Jesus' leadership?

KNOW THE WAY

Some might argue that Jesus didn't need a team. But what He did need was a group of committed teammates who could go out and do the work of spreading His message after He was gone.

One of the best examples of Jesus and the disciples engaging in teamwork can be found in John 6:1-13. Jesus had been teaching a large group of people along the seaside and could sense that they were getting hungry. There was no way they could afford to buy food for everyone, but then Andrew approached Jesus with some news. There was a young boy with five loaves of bread and two fish—but that wasn't nearly enough, right?

> *"Tell everyone to sit down," Jesus said. So they all sat down on the grassy slopes. (The men alone numbered about 5,000.) Then Jesus took the loaves, gave thanks to God, and distributed them to the people. Afterward he did the same with the fish. And they all ate as much as they wanted. After everyone was full, Jesus told his disciples, "Now gather the leftovers, so that nothing is wasted." So they picked up the pieces and filled twelve baskets with scraps left by the people who had eaten from the five barley loaves (vv. 10-13).*

Not only did Jesus demonstrate miraculous faith, He also allowed His disciples to take part in the miracle and work as a team to take care of the people.

At the same time, by having the disciples follow Him, it's possible that Jesus was simply showing us the importance of having teammates to support us throughout our Christian walk.

Q: What characteristics do you look for when considering new friends?

Q: Would you say that your friends are helpful when it comes to the spiritual aspects of your life? Explain.

WRAP UP

If you're ready to take the next step in your faith journey and understand that you can't do it alone, consider these three steps that will help you gain the benefits that come with pursuing a righteous team.

1. **Evaluate the Team:** Decide who will best help you grow in your faith and reach your full potential as a follower of Christ.

   Walk with the wise and become wise; associate with fools and get in trouble (Prov. 13:20).

2. **Draft the Team:** Find those people that can help you, and ask them to be an active part of your faith journey.

   The godly give good advice to their friends; the wicked lead them astray (Prov. 12:26).

3. **Commit to the Team:** Be accountable to those on your team and to your Christian leaders who want to help you. Stay committed to the process. Listen to their advice and follow it to the best of your ability.

   Get all the advice and instruction you can, so you will be wise the rest of your life (Prov. 19:20).

OVERTIME

Just like athletes need to have the right teammates to achieve the greatest success, believers also need to have the right teammates to help them grow stronger in their relationship with Christ. In other words, answering the question of who we have in our lives is essential.

The apostle Paul gives us a great example of what it looks like when we surround ourselves with the right kind of spiritual teammates in Hebrews 10:24-25.

> *"Let us think of ways to motivate one another to acts of love and good works. And let us not neglect our meeting together, as some people do, but encourage one another, especially now that the day of his return is drawing near" (Heb. 10:24-25).*

The question then becomes: who should we be pursuing, and where should we be looking to find them? Using the spaces provided below, put a check mark by the attributes you think would be most important in a Christian teammate.

Compassionate	_____	Malicious	_____
Confident	_____	Prayerful	_____
Inconsistent	_____	Prideful	_____
Jealous	_____	Trustworthy	_____
Judgmental	_____	Truthful	_____
Kind	_____		

Q: List some places where you think you can find Christian teammates with these desirable attributes.

Q: How do you think having teammates with these desirable attributes will help you grow in your Christian walk?

Flip to page 77 and list the names of some people that you would like to be on your spiritual dream team. Map out a plan to draft your team and what steps you will take to commit yourself to the process of being a part of that team. Ask them to go through the Pursue Reading Plan with you on YouVersion by downloading and choosing the "With Friends" feature.

PURSUE EXCELLENCE

"So whether you eat or drink, or whatever you do, do it all for the glory of God."

1 Corinthians 10:31

———————

Q: What represents excellence in your sport?

Q: What motivates you to give your best as an athlete?

WATCH SESSION 7 VIDEO

WORKOUT

A TALE OF TWO MOTIVES

In Session 3, we talked about the broader goal or the "why" behind our desire to pursue a particular path in life. But let's drill down into something even more specific—defining the "why" behind our desire (or motivation) to pursue excellence, which is one of the biggest drives for athletes.

To see what the Bible has to say about the motivation for excellence, we can take a look at the short but powerful story that took place not long before Jesus' death and resurrection. Jesus and the disciples were on their way to Jerusalem when they stopped in a village where a woman named Martha invited them into her home. Her sister, Mary, was also there and spent her time listening to Jesus teach.

> *But Martha was distracted by the big dinner she was preparing. She came to Jesus and said, "Lord, doesn't it seem unfair to you that my sister just sits here while I do all the work? Tell her to come and help me." But the Lord said to her, "My dear Martha, you are worried and upset over all these details! There is only one thing worth being concerned about. Mary has discovered it, and it will not be taken away from her"* (Luke 10:40-42).

Martha wasn't doing anything inherently wrong. There was a need to get things done around the house and prepare for the guests. She was focused on the right things but in the wrong order. Her motivation was misplaced. Martha was pursuing excellence for the sake of perfection. She was driven by the need to please others with her works.

Mary, on the other hand, had a different motivation. Her excellence was exhibited in the outpouring of her desire to be in relationship with Jesus. That was the purest form of worship that she could give in that moment.

Q: When you're training to reach your athletic goals, how often do you think about the motivation behind your hard work?

Q: Why do you think Jesus needed to differentiate between Martha and Mary's choices? How do these differences help you understand what excellence should look like?

KNOW THE GOAL

As Christian athletes, it's important to make sure we understand the goal behind our pursuit of godly excellence. Excellence is what leads us to the goal. Winning is good, but it's not the ultimate goal. Our ultimate goal for anything we do in life is to worship and glorify God and to exemplify Christ. That's what our excellence is really meant to achieve.

The goal is not perfection—that's impossible.

The goal is not winning—you might give your best and still come up short.

The goal is not pleasing others—you'll never please everyone.

The goal is not pleasing you—achievement won't fulfill you.

The goal is to worship God through your best efforts, give Him the glory no matter the result, and use the opportunity to reveal to others that Christ is living in you. True worship is not compartmentalized, so for athletes, this means focusing on Jesus before, during, and after competition. The apostle Paul often wrote about this in his letters to the early church:

> And so, dear brothers and sisters, I plead with you to give your bodies to God because of all he has done for you. Let them be a living and holy sacrifice—the kind he will find acceptable. This is truly the way to worship him (Rom. 12:1).

> Therefore, let us offer through Jesus a continual sacrifice of praise to God, proclaiming our allegiance to his name (Heb. 13:15).

Not only did Jesus demonstrate miraculous faith, He also allowed them to take part in the miracle and work as a team to take care of the people.

> So whether you eat or drink, or whatever you do, do it all for the glory of God (1 Cor. 10:31).

Q: How much does winning or athletic success motivate you? Why do think that's the case?

Q: List some ways you can glorify Christ when you achieve athletic success.

Q: How can glorify Christ when you fall short of your athletic goals?

Surrendering your athletic pursuits to Christ isn't easy. As we discussed in Session 4, being an athlete is deeply embedded into our identity and can be difficult to release. However, once we understand how much more God has for us and how much He has already done for us, we can shift our motivations for excellence from pleasing ourselves and others into the more fulfilling desire to please Him above anyone else.

Here are three ways to help make that become a reality in your life:

1. **Check Your Motives:** Be honest about what is driving you to give your best. Ask yourself the difficult questions about your motivation. Ask close friends to help you see things you might have overlooked. And ultimately, ask the Holy Spirit to reveal your true motives so you can begin the process of reprioritizing your efforts.

   Search me, O God, and know my heart; test me and know my anxious thoughts. Point out anything in me that offends you, and lead me along the path of everlasting life (Ps. 139:23-24).

2. **Shift Your Focus:** Take your eyes off yourself, your personal goals, and pleasing others, and put your focus on God above everything else.

   Since you have been raised to new life with Christ, set your sights on the realities of heaven, where Christ sits in the place of honor at God's right hand. Think about the things of heaven, not the things of earth. For you died to this life, and your real life is hidden with Christ in God. And when Christ, who is your life, is revealed to the whole world, you will share in all his glory (Col. 3:1-4).

3. **Give Your Best:** Commit to being excellent in training, in competition, in your sportsmanship, in your relationships, and in your service to God and others. Do all of these things first and foremost to please God while trusting that He will take care of the results and get you where you need to be.

   Work willingly at whatever you do, as though you were working for the Lord rather than for people. Remember that the Lord will give you an inheritance as your reward, and that the Master you are serving is Christ (Col. 3:23-24).

OVERTIME

Athletic pursuits are naturally tied toward inwardly focused motivations and goals. That's what makes it so difficult for us to shift our focus away from ourselves and onto the higher purpose of worshiping and glorifying God through our drive for excellence.

Using the scenarios below, come up with some examples of how certain aspects of your athletic pursuits can be focused on thinking about yourself or others (inward focus), and then determine a way that you can refocus that attention on worshipping and glorifying God (upward focus).

	Inward Focus	Upward Focus
Physical Training	_____	_____
Practice Time	_____	_____
Peer Interaction	_____	_____
Authority Interaction	_____	_____
Pregame Preparation	_____	_____
Competitive Effort	_____	_____
Opponent Interaction	_____	_____
Competitive Success	_____	_____
Competitive Failure	_____	_____
Postgame Response	_____	_____

Q: Which of these areas is most difficult for you to take the focus off of yourself or pleasing others? Why do think that's the case?

Q: How can you redirect your focus away from yourself and onto God during these various aspects of athletic training and competition?

Q: In what ways might refocusing on God during your athletic pursuits impact your ability to give your best on a consistent basis?

PURSUE MISSION

"But you will receive power when the Holy Spirit comes upon you. And you will be my witnesses, telling people about me everywhere—in Jerusalem, throughout Judea, in Samaria, and to the ends of the earth."

Acts 1:8

_____

WARM-UP

Q: What are some ways that an athlete can be selfish: "more about me and less about we"?

Q: List some examples of how an athlete can shift from inward pursuits (doing things for themselves) to outward pursuits (doing things for others).

WATCH SESSION 8 VIDEO

WORKOUT

NOBODY SPECIAL

Athletes aren't the only ones who have dreams of leaving a legacy and working toward a greater good. In fact, the Bible has many great examples of people who experienced a paradigm shift in their lives and began to see a much bigger picture of what the future held in store for them.

In Session 6, we talked about how Jesus put a team together so He could teach and train them to take and spread His message to the world. But before they were Jesus' teammates, they were ordinary people from ordinary backgrounds.

Andrew, Peter, James, and John were fishermen. Matthew was a tax collector. The other disciples' occupations apparently weren't exciting or impressive enough to even be mentioned. Yet, Jesus chose these people to accomplish His great mission.

And the results were world changing. In the Book of Acts, you can read about all of the amazing things they accomplished during their time on Earth. They started the Christian church, converted thousands of people to the Christian faith, and performed amazing miracles—just like Jesus said they would.

> *"I tell you the truth, anyone who believes in me will do the same works I have done, and even greater works, because I am going to be with the Father" (John 14:12).*

It was like a coach taking a bunch of underrated recruits and turning them into a championship team! And it was all because they accepted a much greater mission instead of settling for the lives they had once known.

Q: Why do you think the disciples could do such great things after Jesus left Earth?

Q: How does their story inspire you as a follower of Christ?

KNOW THE WHERE

We all need greater purpose and meaning in our lives. Oftentimes, it's the search for that purpose and meaning that leads us down the wrong path. But everything changes when we finally understand that our mission is ultimately tied to a relationship with Christ.

That's because our walk with Him is inseparable from the calling that we all receive from Him, which is the same calling that Jesus gave the disciples.

> *Jesus came and told his disciples, "I have been given all authority in heaven and on earth. Therefore, go and make disciples of all the nations, baptizing them in the name of the Father and the Son and the Holy Spirit. Teach these new disciples to obey all the commands I have given you. And be sure of this: I am with you always, even to the end of the age" (Matt. 28:18-20).*

We often struggle to understand where we should go and what we should do. But Jesus gave us a clear mission to share the gospel with our world and help others grow in their relationships with Him. When we understand that God holds our future in His hands, that's when we go beyond our ordinary lives and risk everything to tell the world about Jesus.

Q: How is our calling in life tied directly to our relationship with Christ?

Q: What are some things that might be holding you back from accepting God's mission?

WRAP UP

If you're ready to accept God's call, here are three ways that you can begin to pursue mission and start walking in the fullness of what He has laid out for you to do:

1. **Trust the Mission:** Fully embrace what God has called you to do and believe that He will give you everything you need to get the job done.

   ...may he equip you with all you need for doing his will. May he produce in you, through the power of Jesus Christ, every good thing that is pleasing to him. All glory to him forever and ever! Amen (Heb. 13:21).

2. **Prepare for the Mission:** Getting ready to do God's work is no different than getting ready for athletic competition. It requires diligent preparation through consistent prayer, Bible reading, and Christian fellowship.

   All athletes are disciplined in their training. They do it to win a prize that will fade away, but we do it for an eternal prize. So I run with purpose in every step. I am not just shadowboxing. I discipline my body like an athlete, training it to do what it should. Otherwise, I fear that after preaching to others I myself might be disqualified (1 Cor. 9:25-27).

3. **Commit to the Mission:** Make the decision that you will not give up even when things get tough.

   So, my dear brothers and sisters, be strong and immovable. Always work enthusiastically for the Lord, for you know that nothing you do for the Lord is ever useless (1 Cor. 15:58).

OVERTIME

How did the disciples do the great things after Jesus left the earth? They did it because of what Jesus left behind for them—a powerful tool that gives them the ability to accomplish great things.

> *"But you will receive power when the Holy Spirit comes upon you. And you will be my witnesses, telling people about me everywhere— in Jerusalem, throughout Judea, in Samaria, and to the ends of the earth" (Acts 1:8).*

And this is the same way that you can embark on the most meaningful mission you could ever imagine—an unstoppable mission that God calls all of us to accept.

Q: What are some things that you want to do with your life that you consider to be bigger than yourself?

Q: Does the idea of pursuing God's mission for your life excite you, scare you, or not interest you at all? Explain.

Using the space below, write down five missions you feel like you might be called to pursue immediately and/or in the future:

1.

2.

3.

4.

5.

Share these ideas with someone in your life that you trust (e.g., parent, coach, teacher, pastor, etc.), and ask them for advice on how you can start to pursue missions today.

LEADER
GUIDE TIPS

LEADER GUIDE TIPS

PRAY DILIGENTLY

Ask God to prepare you to lead this study. Pray individually and specifically for the students in your group. Make this a priority in your personal walk and preparation. Also, prepare for each group session with prayer. Ask the Holy Spirit to work through you and the group discussion as you point to Jesus each week through God's Word.

PREPARE ADEQUATELY

Don't just wing this. Take time to preview each session so you have a good grasp of the content. Look over the group session and consider your students. Feel free to delete or reword the questions provided, and add other questions that fit your group better. Students will need a Bible study book, so consider keeping a few extras on hand for students who join later. Also, suggest students bring a Bible and journal to group each week.

INCLUDE OTHERS

Your goal is to foster a community that welcomes students just as they are, but also encourages them to grow spiritually. Always be aware of opportunities to include anyone who visits the group and invite new people to join.

ENCOURAGE FREELY

Cheer for your students and encourage them to participate in every part of the study.

LEAD BY EXAMPLE

Make sure you complete all of the personal study. Be willing to share your story, what you're learning, and your questions as you discuss together.

BE AWARE

If students are hesitant to discuss their thoughts and questions in a larger group, consider dividing into smaller groups to provide a setting more conducive to conversation.

KEEP CONNECTING

Think of ways to connect with students during the week. If a student mentions a prayer request or need, make sure to follow up. Participation always improves when members spend time connecting with one another outside the group sessions. The more people are comfortable with and involved in one another's lives, the more they'll look forward to being together.

EVALUATE OFTEN

After each session and throughout the study, assess what needs to be changed to more effectively lead the study.

TRAINING TIME
DEVOS

DEVO ONE

READY

> *They traded the truth about God for a lie. So they worshiped and served the things God created instead of the Creator himself, who is worthy of eternal praise! Amen (Rom. 1:25).*

SET

In the 2012 Women's College World Series, Alabama had just beaten Oklahoma to win the National Title. Coach Patty Gasso of Oklahoma asked me to come down on the field and address the team after this huge loss. What could I say to a team that had just lost the National Title? The truth. As we sat there on the field with Alabama in a winning dog-pile beside us, the truth was spoken. The truth was that losing is hard and hurts. The truth was that, "you have shown an entire country who you praise when you win. Now, you have the chance to show an entire country who you praise when you lose." And they did exactly that. From their loss in 2012 to their win in 2013, the team put Jesus front and center in their press conferences and interviews, knowing that every blessing that doesn't turn into praise turns into pride.

As athletes, we are told that our talents and abilities should be the central focus and truth of anything we do, but that is a lie! The truth is we should make a platform for Christ and Christ alone. When we pursue Him, we will find the truth of who God is, what God has done, and who God has called us to be as Christian athletes.

GO

1. List some truths you know about God.

2. In what ways do you believe the lies of the world instead of the truth of God?

3. How can we pursue the truth of God as athletes?

WORKOUT

John 6:47; 14:6; Ephesians 6:14

DEVO TWO

READY

> *O Lord, I have longed for your rescue, and your instructions are my delight. Let me live so I can praise you, and may your regulations help me. I have wandered away like a lost sheep; come and find me, for I have not forgotten your commands (Ps. 119:174-176).*

SET

My dad loved to engage with God daily. He was a passionate man who loved to challenge people to have a daily quiet time. Even though he passed away last year after a long fight with leukemia, his passion impacted thousands. It was a passion that overflowed from him because it was such an essential part of his life. But it had not always been that way. Eighteen years ago he was an overcommitted businessman who would squeeze in a quick two-minute devotion in his car before heading into the office.

That all changed with a man named Brad Curl. He saw that my dad was skimming when it came to his devotions. Brad decided to communicate in a way that got my dad's attention. Brad literally grabbed him by the collar and said, "Ed, you need to stop playing with God. You are a Christian leader, and you need to start diving into God's Word and getting serious! No more giving God leftovers!" As a very intense person himself, my dad responded to this style of communication. That day marked my dad. No more playing. He started digging in. My dad's life began to transform, and as he spent time in the Bible, the Bible seeped into his life.

Jesus Christ is waiting today to empower you with His presence. It is not easy, but it's worth it. Stay with it until it becomes a delight. It is a delight for the Lord Jesus Christ every day when I engage Him even if it starts out feeling like a chore for me. He longs to be with you. Engage God today.

GO

1. What is getting in the way of making daily devotions a part of your life? List all the things that prevent you from getting into the Word.

2. Accountability is key. Do you have a Brad Curl in your life who can speak truth into you?

3. How does it make you feel knowing that God delights in you every time you engage with Him? It is never drudgery or discipline for Him.

WORKOUT

Psalm 1:2; 35:9; 2 Peter 1:3-11

DEVO THREE

READY

> *We are pressed on every side by troubles, but we are not crushed. We are perplexed, but not driven to despair. We are hunted down, but never abandoned by God. We get knocked down, but we are not destroyed (2 Cor. 4:8-9).*

SET

One of the most upsetting things about sports is when athletes get injured. To see someone on the sidelines is contrary to the image of athleticism. It can feel miserable when we are that athlete. Yet every athlete who performs their sport does so with the knowledge there are inherent risks.

The reality is that every one of us has limitations because we are born into a fallen world, surrounded by wounded people. We are personally fractured, but the solution to the problem isn't Christianity. Entering into relationship with Christ ensures of us of salvation. But if we think, or allow others to think, that means we will never suffer, we will be disappointed. God forgives sin, but we often have to deal with the result of sin. The entire world is still experiencing the consequences brought on by Adam and Eve's disobedience. People who blame God for the condition of this world don't understand this truth. The assurance is of peace in the midst of trouble. Peace is available. Trouble is guaranteed.

A dedicated athlete doesn't give up a sport even though wounds are a possibility, just as Christians shouldn't give up when life gets tough. It is too easy to take skills and people for granted in this life. When something we treasure is threatened or taken from us, we start to approach life much differently. If you are being tempted to walk away from sports, academics, a job, a relationship or God because of tough times, please reconsider. Things are not always what they seem in the moment.

GO

1. In what areas of your life are you facing the most challenges?

2. Do you spend more time talking about your problems than in prayer about them?

3. What trusted friend can help you navigate through tough times?

WORKOUT

John 16:33; 2 Corinthians 1:3-4; 4:18

DEVO FOUR

READY

> What sorrow awaits those who look to Egypt for help, trusting their
> horses, chariots, and charioteers and depending on the strength of
> human armies instead of looking to the Lord, the Holy One of Israel
> (Isa. 31:1).

SET

My first fall playing collegiate Division I volleyball went exactly as I imagined.
We became conference champions and competed in the NCAA tournament.
It was smooth sailing. Though classes were difficult and I was homesick, I
found comfort in the 900 square-foot volleyball court that was the same
it had always been. My second year started like the first. However, six
starters had graduated. After our first win, the season disintegrated. As a
sophomore, I could no longer hide behind the older players.

Suddenly, that court didn't look as familiar. We began that season as
conference champions and ended with a 5-25 record. At the season's end,
all I could think about was my failure as a player and anger toward the
game. Later I understood that God had deliberately sought my submission.
Proverbs 3:5-6 states, "Trust in the Lord with all your heart; do not depend
on your own understanding. Seek his will in all you do, and he will show
you which path to take." I hadn't trusted God. I had trusted my abilities,
teammates, and coaches.

"Jesus Christ is the same yesterday, today, and forever" (Heb. 13:8). And
although we cannot rely on the outcome of games or seasons, we can rely
on God.

GO

1. Has a coach or teammate ever let you down? How so?

2. How can you be more self-controlled next time you face disappointment?

3. Have you ever trusted in your own abilities over trusting God's plan?

WORKOUT

Psalm 9:9-10; Isaiah 26:3-4; Jeremiah 17:7

DEVO FIVE

PURSUE LIFE // *SHANTA CRICHLOW*

READY

> But for us, There is one God, the Father, by whom all things were created, and for whom we live. And there is one Lord, Jesus Christ, through whom all things were created, and through whom we live (1 Cor. 8:6).

SET

As a high school and college track athlete, Jesus was my competitive edge. I read Scripture before every meet and believed that being a Christian would translate into good athletic performances. When I was diagnosed with cancer and my track and field career ended with one year of eligibility remaining, Jesus was my comfort. Before, I pursued Christ for what I could get out of the relationship with Him. But I found that there's so much more to it than that.

There's a reason you said "yes" to Jesus that is special and unique to you. Perhaps you said "yes" to help you become a better player or coach, heal a broken heart, secure a good future, or have eternal life. The truth is, each of our journeys began the same way. God chose us: "For no one can come to me unless the Father who sent me draws them to me, and at the last day I will raise them up" (John 6:44).

We pursue our sport for the many things we can get out of it, such as glory, fame, fun, and so on. We pursue Christ because of who He is, all He's done for us, and the fact that He loved us first. We have life through Him! Pursuing life surrendered to Christ is how we say, "Thank You."

GO

1. What first inspired you to say "yes" to Jesus?

2. How has an unanswered prayer changed your relationship with God?

3. Which traits of Christ inspire you to continue pursuing life with Him today?

WORKOUT

John 1:4; Acts 17:28; 1 Corinthians 8:6; Colossians 1:16

DEVO SIX

THE COST OF LOVE // *ROGER LIPE*

READY

> For this is how God loved the world: He gave his one and only Son,
> so that everyone who believes in him will not perish but have eternal
> life. God sent his Son into the world not to judge the world, but to
> save the world through him (John 3:16-17).

SET

Imagine that your best teammates, ones with whom you have built strong
relationships of love and respect, were suddenly separated from you by a
rebellious act of betrayal. How would you feel? How could you ever restore
those relationships after they had suffered such a crushing loss?

That's similar to how God must have felt, and continues to feel, due to our
rebellion and betrayal of Him. His heart is grieved by our sinful rejection of
His love. How would He restore His relationship with us?

The great news is that He sent Jesus to Earth, while we were still in our
rebellion and rejecting His love, to live, to die, and to rise again to fully
restore our relationship with God. Even more, He promises us life beyond the
grave, eternally in His presence. That's amazing!

Take a moment to think about the depth and power of God's love. His love
pays the price to restore us to a loving relationship with Him through our
belief in Jesus Christ.

GO

1. What do you love about sports? What have you sacrificed for your sport?

2. Which relationships are most important to you? What would you be
willing to sacrifice should those relationships be suddenly broken?

3. How will you respond to God's gift of sacrifice to restore your relationship
with Him?

WORKOUT

John 1:12; Romans 3:23; 5:8

DEVO SEVEN

READY

> There are "friends" who destroy each other, but a real friend sticks closer than a brother (Prov. 18:24).

SET

If I asked you to name one person on your team that you consider a brother or sister, could you answer me? What about a teammate that is a real friend? Truth is, we all have that one teammate that instantly comes to mind. This teammate is trustworthy, genuine, supportive, a team player, loving, encouraging, uplifting, and a really good listener. This teammate is a friend that walks by our side and leads us to a life full of positivity, accountability, and brotherly and sisterly love. I believe this is the type of friend Proverbs 18:24 is speaking of—a friend who sticks closer than a brother or sister.

When someone uses "air quotes" around a word, that usually indicates sarcasm. Proverbs is comparing the difference of "friends" and real friends. It's important to pursue and surround yourself with the real friends in life— the ones who lead you to Christ and stick by your side. Friendship is truly life shaping, so it is vital that we pursue Christlike friendships. Along with pursuing real friends, it's just as important to be a real friend and a real teammate to others. Pursue being the one who sticks closer than a brother or sister. Be a real friend, not a "friend." Be the teammate that is wise, bold in their faith, and leads others to Christ. This type of friend is who God wants us to be.

Remember that question I asked in the first sentence? If that question was asked to one of your teammates, would they respond with your name?

GO

1. Describe the difference between a real friend and a "friend."

2. How can you be a real teammate?

3. Why does God want us to pursue friends who are real?

WORKOUT

Proverbs 27:17; John 15:13

DEVO EIGHT

READY

> Love never gives up, never loses faith, is always hopeful, and
> endures through every circumstance (1 Cor. 13:7).

SET

As athletes, we know what it means to be challenged: to push past our limits
and train hard in every practice. Sports are not easy, and we know that
growth and improvement only come by working hard and strengthening our
weaknesses. There comes a moment when every athlete gets discouraged.
We hit a wall, lose our hope in improvement, and lose our faith to grow.
These are the days that it would be easier to quit, to let discouragement
or fear overcome our mind, and give up. It is also in these days that we
desperately need to be deeply encouraged and lifted up.

I have often heard the well-known phrase, "Never give up!" This small
quote is intended to be inspiring and is placed on posters in locker rooms,
on t-shirts, and notebooks, but what does it really mean? Who or what or
how should I never give up? God tells us in His Word that God's perfect
love never gives up. God does not give up loving you, and He has chosen to
endure every circumstance with you.

There will be days when all we can think of is giving up, but as Christians,
we can be encouraged that God loves us. He will never give up on us and
chooses to walk through life with us. He gives us the strength we need to
keep the faith and endure through every discouragement.

GO

1. Can you remember a time when you were so discouraged that you wanted
to give up?

2. What does love that "never gives up" mean to you?

3. How will depending on God's enduring love change the way you play
and train?

WORKOUT

Isaiah 41:10; Ephesians 6:10

DEVO NINE

READY

> *For in Christ lives all the fullness of God in a human body. So you also are complete through your union with Christ, who is the head over every ruler and authority (Col. 2:9-10).*

SET

The world's definition of excellence is based on performance. As soon as you're not performing, no one in the media wants to talk to you anymore, and it's easy to get down on yourself. Excellence is all wrapped up in performance. It's like building your house on sand. This definition of excellence is very changing and fleeting, and eventually, it's going to be gone because no one is always on top of his or her game. When you find your identity in Christ and in what He's done for you, that truth is the unchanging, sturdy rock that you can always stand on.

When I'm not performing well, I lose my hope. I lose my joy. I get down. I get depressed. But when you find your identity in Christ, that's unchanging. No matter what you do, you can't mess that up. Excellence is getting back up after you've fallen. It's knowing that your true value is in Christ and that He is our hope for the future. He is our everything. This truth is not based on performance.

GO

1. How does your athletic performance affect your emotions and your attitude?

2. Which words do you like to be identified by as an athlete? Why are those descriptions important to you?

3. What does the phrase "find your identity in Christ" mean to you? How might accepting the premise of Colossians 2:9-10 change the way you approach performance?

WORKOUT

John 14:12; 15:15; Romans 8:15-17

DEVO TEN

READY

> See how very much our Father loves us, for he calls us his children, and that is what we are! But the people who belong to this world don't recognize that we are God's children because they don't know him (1 John 3:1).

SET

While Bill Russell was playing with the NBA championship team the Boston Celtics, he was once stopped in an airport and asked if he was a basketball player. He replied, "No, basketball is what I do, not who I am." Competing is what you do, not who you are.

Who you are must be bigger than any role in your life. Confusing your role with your identity will have a couple of negative results. First, you will be tempted to link your value as a person to your performances. You will play horribly and think you have lost your value. Second, the loss of your role can be devastating if you equate your role with your identity—if you think people value you only when you compete.

Instead, define who you are beyond what you do. Ultimately, to know who you are, you must know whose you are. You belong to the Lord and are valuable because He created you. Yes, it hurts to perform poorly and to lose a big game, but your performance does not define who you are.

You are not a competitor who just happens to be a Christian; you are a Christian who just happens to be a competitor.

GO

1. How have you let what you do define who you are?

2. Do you feel like you have more personal worth after a win or less after a loss? Why might that not be a good thing?

3. How can God's view of you change the way you compete and live?

WORKOUT

1 Corinthians 6:19-20; 2 Corinthians 5:17; 1 Peter 2:9

DEVO ELEVEN

DARE TO BE DIFFERENT // *RICK ISAIAH*

READY

> But you are not like that, for you are a chosen people. You are royal priests, a holy nation, God's very own possession. As a result, you can show others the goodness of God, for he called you out of the darkness into his wonderful light (1 Pet. 2:9).

SET

It has been proven that even identical twins have different DNA. If that is the case, what is God telling us about our uniqueness? I believe He is telling us to be different: not to conform to the world's standards; to be in the world but not of the world. I know this is difficult and seems to be a paradox, especially in a world where we are told to be a team player or to play, coach, or live for our own agendas.

God does expect us to be a team player, yet He calls us to be different at the same time. In football, everyone wears the same uniform, but has different responsibilities. We are the body of Christ, one team, united under the blood-stained banner, but we all have different responsibilities and gifts. First Peter 2:9 gives us guidance on daring to be different. As we read that passage, we see that we are all on one team—in the world but not of the world—and that we are called to be different. God's guidance on being different includes:

- **Selected:** God chose you to be different from everyone else.
- **Servant:** God called you to service.
- **Sanctified:** God set you apart for an eternal purpose.
- **Zealous:** We should be excited to be on His team—the winning team!

GO

1. How are you playing differently from your peers?

2. Are you playing Christ's way no matter what?

3. Are you spending time with God daily to hear His instructions and gain His strength so you can stand firm?

WORKOUT

John 17:12-17; Colossians 4:11-12; 1 Peter 4:9-11

DEVO TWELVE

READY

> *I want them to be encouraged and knit together by strong ties of love. I want them to have complete confidence that they understand God's mysterious plan, which is Christ himself (Col. 2:2).*

SET

Our world has been turned upside down. The rhythm and routines of our daily life have been disrupted, and everyone has been affected. For coaches and athletes, seasons have ended abruptly. Many workers and parents' lives have been thrown into confusion and disarray.

Even when we don't have answers and have difficulty understanding what's going on in our world, we can be encouraged in our hearts. God's Word affirms that!

Several years ago, an athlete training for an Ironman event was hospitalized with a severe staff infection. Shock and disappointment came when the doctors told him he was done for the season. He had trained and planned not just to compete, but to beat his personal best time. As he laid in the hospital after hearing the news, God revealed to him that the race had become his central focus. He quietly surrendered the race to God, regained his focus, and was encouraged in his heart by his heavenly Father.

When we are facing difficult times and major setbacks, we don't need answers, we need Jesus! Paul's goal in writing to the Colossian church was to encourage their hearts so they would know God's plan, which is Christ. He has all the answers. We simply need to live for Him and in Him, strengthened in faith and overflowing with gratitude for His comfort and love.

GO

1. What can you do today to recalibrate and regain a focus on Christ?

2. How can you encourage the heart of a teammate or coach today?

3. How do you react when your plans abruptly change?

WORKOUT

Colossians 2:6-7; 3:1-3; 2 Peter 3:9-11

DEVO THIRTEEN

THE ULTIMATE STANDARD // COREY STEELE

READY

> *For I fully expect and hope that I will never be ashamed, but that I will continue to be bold for Christ, as I have been in the past. And I trust that my life will bring honor to Christ, whether I live or die (Phil 1:20).*

SET

As a coach or an athlete, we face daily expectations and standards for developing a winning program and performing at a high level. In most cases, the bigger the program, the bigger the expectations. Being a student athlete or college coach, the pressure may be multiplied due to the demand of those assigned over you. The pressure to meet standards set by our coaches, parents, peers, and colleagues can weigh heavy at times. The fear of disappointment can be a huge obstacle that may hinder decision-making capability and performance. Sometimes, we place more pressure on ourselves than any outside source.

When faced with the pressure of expectations and standards, you can turn to the One who sets the ultimate standard. Jesus is the perfect standard. Knowing who you are in Christ and developing your relationship with Him accomplishes the ultimate standard for your life.

Philippians 4:13 says, "For I can do everything through Christ, who gives me strength." Christ set a standard for us to live boldly for God on and off the field, unashamedly. The only standard to live by is God's standard. Nothing else can compare.

GO

1. What expectations do you face daily and how do you approach them?

2. How does the example of Christ show you how to live for God?

3. How can your life reflect a godly standard on and off the field?

WORKOUT

Isaiah 59:17; Galatians 2:20; 3:29; Philippians 4:13

DEVO FOURTEEN

THE HIGHEST GOAL // *ALICIA CARDIE*

READY

> Let love be your highest goal! But you should also desire the special abilities the Spirit gives—especially the ability to prophesy (1 Cor. 14:1).

SET

I think nearly every kid in sports dreams about going to the Olympics someday. To earn a spot to compete at the highest level, representing an entire nation, pursuing the glory and honor that comes with winning a gold medal—it's an awe-inspiring feeling. And for many, it becomes an all-consuming goal.

But God doesn't tell us to set the Olympics as our highest goal. Actually, as Christians, we're already in a sort of divine Olympics: we've been given gifts of the highest level by God Himself, we're representing His entire kingdom, and we're pursuing His glory. To drive that whole pursuit, God tells us that love is our highest goal. Not money. Not a medal. Not fame. But love.

As we train and compete every day and simply go about our lives, we face hundreds of decisions, and what we choose will paint a very clear picture of what we're striving toward. It becomes evident in how we act, how we relate to others, and what we do with our time. Every day, above all else, we should be choosing love.

GO

1. What was or is your biggest sports goal growing up or right now?

2. What kind of decisions do you make every day? What do these decisions tell others about what you value?

3. How can you choose to make love your highest goal this week?

WORKOUT

Matthew 20:25-28; Ephesians 5:2

DEVO FIFTEEN

READY

> *And let us not neglect our meeting together, as some people do, but encourage one another, especially now that the day of his return is drawing near (Heb. 10:25).*

SET

When we make a mental error or slack off in our effort, we expect to be yelled at by a coach; but when a teammate yells at you, or even puts you down, it can really hurt. I remember this happening during little league baseball in sixth grade. I was made fun of a lot for my glasses, height, and weight, among other things. Plus, I simply wasn't good at baseball, which did not help. After two or three practices, I told my mom I wasn't going back. I hated quitting, but not having any support on my own team was worse. A little encouragement might have been the difference between me finishing the season and quitting.

More than once in the book of Hebrews, it says we are to encourage one another. Sharing a kind word with someone could make a difference. Putting an arm around a friend who is hurting could make a difference. Even a smile, hug, or handshake could make a huge difference in another's direction, and maybe even their life.

Hebrews 10:24-25 says it plainly: "Let us think of ways to motivate one another to acts of love and good works. And let us not neglect our meeting together, as some people do, but encourage one another, especially now that the day of his return is drawing near."

So, let's motivate one another to do good things. Let's keep getting together and enjoying others. Let's encourage one another with thoughtful, kind words and attitudes, and let's show others an example of Jesus by exhibiting kindness to all those around us.

GO

1. Have you ever been put down by a teammate? How did it feel?

2. What can we do if we see teammates putting others down?

3. In step with Hebrews 10:24-25, what could you do to motivate, gather with, or encourage others?

WORKOUT

Romans 14:19; 1 Corinthians 13:4-7

DEVO SIXTEEN

HELPING OTHERS BE GREAT // *SARAH ROBERTS*

READY

> *There is no greater love than to lay down one's life for one's friends (John 15:13).*

SET

In the 90s, I was a huge Chicago Bulls fan—everyone was. We were watching the greatest player in the history of the game, Michael Jordan, make history. Although I loved MJ, my favorite player was the point guard, BJ Armstrong. He wasn't regarded as the star of the team, but he nevertheless helped his teammates achieve success.

Jonathan was the son of King Saul and rightful heir to be the next king of Israel. However, God hadn't chosen him; He chose Jonathan's best friend David. Instead of feeling jealous or robbed of the throne, Jonathan was willing to come alongside David and help him achieve greatness and success. He had many opportunities to turn David over to his father, but he didn't. Instead, Jonathan encouraged David to lead with trust and faith in his heart. In 1 Samuel, we see how Jonathan encourages and empowers him to do just that (1 Sam. 23:16-18).

Even if there's a virus that ends our season or an injury that keeps us from playing, we can all still achieve success by supporting others. Through Jonathan's example, we can learn three important lessons:

1. He practiced humility; it wasn't about him.
2. He accepted where God had him.
3. He was an encourager and empowered his "teammate."

It's the assist that never gets noticed and the block that never gets the credit, but just like God saw Jonathan, God sees you helping your teammates be great, too. How can you help your teammate through his or her struggle today?

GO

1. Who has been a Jonathan teammate to you—willing to come alongside you and encourage you?

2. Which of the above lessons do you need to work on to be a great teammate?

WORKOUT

Philippians 2:3; 1 Peter 4:10

DEVO SEVENTEEN

NO EXCUSES // JIMMY PAGE

READY

> *But they all began making excuses. One said, 'I have just bought a field and must inspect it. Please excuse me' (Luke 14:18).*

SET

When I was 12, I was playing second base for an all-star team. I still remember dropping that pop fly that ended up, in part, costing us the win. I made excuses—blaming the rain and even the lights (it was a night game). At the time, I didn't think I was making excuses; I just didn't want the loss to be my fault.

Excuses spread like a virus. We blame the refs, our teammates, and even the weather! We make excuses for why we're late to practice, why we didn't work out, why we missed a shot—you name it. When we justify why we didn't do what we should've, it's easier to make excuses the next time.

In Luke 14, Jesus exposes excuses. Those who had been invited to the great feast found many excuses for why they couldn't attend, but none of the reasons were genuine.

> *"But they all began making excuses. One said, 'I have just bought a field and must inspect it. Please excuse me.' Another said, 'I have just bought five pairs of oxen, and I want to try them out. Please excuse me.' Another said, 'I just got married, so I can't come'"* (Luke 14:18-20).

Excuses never make you better. And they don't change your circumstances: they solidify them. When excuses become a habit, we're running on a road to failure. These three words are a sure sign of an excuse: could've, would've, and should've. Instead of pointing the finger, we need to take responsibility and assume ownership of the problem. We must own both the problem and the solution. It's time to stop making excuses.

GO

1. Have you ever played the blame game? Why is this so destructive to a team?

2. Do you take personal responsibility, or do you make excuses? Why?

WORKOUT

Luke 6:41-42; 18:9-14; Philippians 2:2-4

Adapted from Jimmy Page and Dan Britton, *True Competitor: 52 Devotions for Athletes, Coaches, and Parents* (Savage, Minnesota: BroadStreet Publishing, 2020).

DEVO EIGHTEEN

READY

> I appeal to you, dear brothers and sisters, by the authority of our Lord Jesus Christ, to live in harmony with each other. Let there be no divisions in the church. Rather, be of one mind, united in thought and purpose (1 Cor. 1:10).

SET

We often see competition as war—a battle to be won over the enemy. Rivalries grow producing "win at any cost" mentalities. It becomes us versus them, good versus evil, winner versus loser. At its origin, the word compete means to "strive together;" to push to a level of play or skill that we cannot attain on our own. Competition does not exist without a partner, whether a teammate or the opposing team. The relationship is complementary, not adversarial.

Let's say there are three first basemen on the softball team. Only one can get the starting nod. Would the other two hope their teammate commits a couple errors and goes 0 to 4 at the plate? Yes, they might hope their teammate fails. Would it be good for the players on the bench? Possibly. Would it be good for the overall team? Definitely not.

This is seen in the New Testament when there was an apparent conflict between the followers of Apollos and Paul. People took sides creating an air of discontent and contempt. They were competing against, not striving with, their fellow believers. The result: any house divided became weaker, not stronger.

Paul addressed the situation by saying, "STOP IT!" He warned them that Christ would not be happy with or put up with these kinds of attitudes. The people needed to unite and help each other as iron sharpens iron. Only then would their impact be the greatest. Whether on the court, at home, or in our churches, we are better together.

GO

1. Do you view your teammates as friend or foe?

2. What would be different if you viewed teammates as allies rather than enemies?

WORKOUT

Proverbs 27:17; Romans 14:1

DEVO NINETEEN

MOTIVATIONAL KEYS // *ROGER LIPE*

READY

> *Let us think of ways to motivate one another to acts of love and good works. And let us not neglect our meeting together, as some people do, but encourage one another, especially now that the day of his return is drawing near (Heb. 10:24-25).*

SET

Some athletes are motivated by challenge, others by the thrill of winning. Others still are provoked to excellence by the fear of losing. What motivates us to compete at our highest levels? How do coaches and teammates stir us to be our best? We're certainly not all wired the same.

Hebrews provides some insight into motivation. There are important parts of Hebrews 10:24 that directly apply to our lives today: (1) "Let us think of ways to motivate one another" implies that real effort is needed to understand each team member. Where motivation is concerned, one size does not fit all. What promotes a great performance in one person may not affect another. One teammate may require a pat on the back, while another may be motivated by a kick in the pants. We must consider what will stir each person most effectively. (2) We know plenty of people who get stirred up, but not toward "love and good works." The idea is not just to stir them, but to motivate them for the success of the team. Let's be aware of the things that help each one achieve at his or her highest level.

As we compete, we must give careful attention to the motivational keys in each of our teammates and find a way to encourage the best possible performance in each one. That is part of being a great teammate, coach, and competitor.

GO

1. What best motivates you to compete at your highest level?

2. What motivates some of your teammates?

3. How can you stir up your teammates to be their best?

WORKOUT

Romans 15:5-6; 1 Thessalonians 5:11

DEVO TWENTY

READY

> *"Seek the Kingdom of God above all else, and live righteously, and he will give you everything you need" (Matt. 6:33).*

SET

Jesus uses very direct and clear language about pursuing mission. He says to pursue the kingdom of God and to live righteously as if it is life's highest priority. He also promises that our needs will be met when we do this.

Pursuing the kingdom of God means seeking God's authority in all areas of life. He has authority to lead us in every facet of our lives: at home, at school, with friends, on the court, field, pitch, track, mat, or in the pool.

To pursue living righteously means seeking to please God with our lives. How we conduct ourselves can be pleasing to God, but only if we are in a relationship with Him through Christ. Our behavior towards our family, friends, teammates, and opponents is pleasing to God when we honor Him and when we are loving toward others.

The wonderful promise of this verse is that our pursuit of living in God's authority and living in a way that pleases Him has a reward that fulfills our needs. We can find great comfort and security in Jesus' promise.

GO

1. What do people around you pursue as their life's highest priority?

2. How would pursuing God's authority as your highest priority change your daily lifestyle?

3. How could pleasing God with the way you live be your highest priority?

WORKOUT

Luke 4:18; Acts 1:8; 13:47

SPIRITUAL DREAM TEAM

THE FOUR

GOD LOVES YOU

God made you and loves you. His love is boundless and unconditional. God is real, and He wants you to personally experience His love and discover His purpose for your life through a relationship with Him.

Genesis 1:27; John 3:16

SIN SEPARATES YOU

Sin damages your relationships with other people and with God. It keeps us from experiencing the fulfilling life that God intends for us. The result: you are eternally separated from God and the life He planned for you.

Isaiah 59:2; Romans 3:23; 6:23

JESUS RESCUES YOU

Jesus died, but He rose to life again. Jesus offers you peace with God and a personal relationship with Him. Through faith in Jesus, you can experience God's love daily, discover your purpose, and have eternal life after death.

Romans 5:8; 1 Corinthians 15:3-8; 1 Peter 3:8

WILL YOU TRUST JESUS?

You choose to trust Jesus when you believe and confess that Jesus is Lord and surrender your life to Him. Are you ready to place your trust in Jesus?

NOTES